Journeys

For Bob Serow,

Cntl best wishes

ALSO BY BARRY L. ZARET

In his other life as a cardiologist at Yale University School of Medicine and Yale New Haven Medical Center, Dr. Barry L. Zaret has authored several medical texts including:

Yale University School of Medicine Heart Book (with M. Moser and L.S. Cohen)

Yale University School of Medicine Guide to Medical Tests (with P.I. Jatlow and L. D. Katz)

Heart Care for Life (with G. J. Subak-Sharpe)

Clinical Nuclear Cardiology: State-of-the-Art and Future Directions (with G. A. Beller)

Nuclear Cardiology: The Basics (with F. J. Wackers and W. Bruni)

JOURNEYS

Poems

Barry L. Zaret

Antrim House

Simsbury, Connecticut

Library of Congress Control Number: 2012938567

ISBN: 978-1-936482-23-8

Printed & bound by Sheridan Books, Inc.

First Edition, 2012

Book design by Rennie McQuilkin

Front cover painting ("The Road from St. Remy to Arles")
by Barry L. Zaret

Author photograph by Harold Shapiro

Antrim House
860.217.0023
AntrimHouse@comcast.net
www.AntrimHouseBooks.com
21 Goodrich Road, Simsbury, CT 06070

In memory of Myrna (Malka Miriam), my wife of 47½ years, my companion, my muse. Her unconditional love, caring and standards of excellence touched all around her; her dignity and courage in the face of unrelenting disease inspired generations.

ACKNOWLEDGMENTS

The following publications first presented these poems, often in earlier versions:

Caduceus: "A Walk in Taormina," "Teach Me," "Snow Dance,"
  "Berkshire Light," "My Father's Kosher Butcher Shop," "Man
  Plans and God Laughs"
Pharos: "The Jewish Home for the Aged"
Long River Run: "When the Sleet Stopped," "Stop and Shop"

"A Walk in Taormina" and "For Primo Levi" were set to music by Joshua Koningsberg and performed in concert at Congregation B'Nai Jacob, Woodbridge, Connecticut.

There are many to whom I am grateful for support during the writing of this volume. My late wife Myrna urged me to begin writing poetry again; she listened to and critiqued each poem until illness clouded her sensorium. As with my other journeys, she was the quiet driving force behind my accomplishments. Dr. Sherwin (Shep) Nuland reviewed many poems, always providing insightful comments and much encouragement. Rabbi Rick and Judy Eisenberg and Tommy Williams patiently listened to many poems in varying stages of completion. Rennie McQuilkin made invaluable editorial suggestions as the manuscript took its current form. My assistant Astrid Swanson helped in the preparation of this volume with the same meticulousness and patience shown during over 20 years of working together on numerous scientific publications.

I have been blessed with the love and support of my family throughout this journey: my children Adam and Peg, Elliot and Zoë, Owen and Abbie, and my grandchildren Jordan, Brooke, Isaac, Oriana, Solomon and Alexandra. They mean more to me than I can express in words. Recently Renée Schwartz Drell entered my life with warmth, love and understanding that have propelled me forward to personal rebirth and renewed creativity. For this gift I am thankful.

TABLE OF CONTENTS

JOURNEYS

I. PREFACE

TINGLES

Tingles start in my toes,
rise quickly through trunk
to fingers, then scalp.
Afferent nerves
pulsate joyously,
bombarding a brain
receptive to new perceptions.
It's not clear what provokes
this strange feeling.
Perhaps sun
illuminating pond ripples,
snow on hemlock,
a patient's comment,
a moment of love.

Whatever the cause
this is undeniable:
when tingles come
words follow.

II. A JEWISH LIFE

MY FATHER'S KOSHER
BUTCHER SHOP

For years my father served
the Jewish families of Far Rockaway
from behind the counter
of his little butcher shop.
His large following
traveled miles
for ritually proper meat,
ladies first previewing
the small outer window display,
then entering the cold store
to order, bargain, schmooze.
He glided with tango grace
on the sawdust-covered floor,
smiling, cajoling, humoring,
slicing, weighing, wrapping,
carrying large slabs of meat
in muscular forearms
from the store's rear
walk-in refrigerator.
Cap on his head,
cigarette never far away,
pencil behind his ear,
bill added on
brown paper bag.
Thursday stretched
from well before dawn,
until late in the evening.
After *Shabbat* dinner
he collapsed

and slept enough that night
for the whole week.
He worked so very hard,
scratched out a living,
was cheated by his partner.
Devastated, he
sold the store, but
never lost his spirit.

Occasionally I delivered orders,
or just helped out.
When I started college,
the store supplied
my chemistry lab attire,
a long butcher's coat.
New, pristinely white,
untouched by calf blood,
it served me well
while mixing reagents
and precipitating salts.
When accepted to
medical school
with scholarship,
I was headlined:
"Butcher's Boy Makes Good."
My father beamed;
I liked the alliteration;
my friends thought it hilarious.
But they never looked inside
this loving butcher whose
youth far from Rockaway's shore
contained enough pain
to fill fifty lives,

a hurtful montage of
pogrom, orphanhood,
hunger, poverty, betrayal,
care of two young sisters,
travel to foreign lands.
A forgiving butcher,
gentle and wise,
wearing his scars
but not consumed by them,
living his immigrant dream
when his only son was called doctor.
I was proud to be this butcher's boy.

FOR LEW HERMAN

1940-2009

In winter we cleared snow
from the playground court
with our mothers' brooms.
We ran from hoop to hoop,
youngsters transplanted
from Brooklyn and Bronx
to Rockaway's shore,
legs churning, elbows
flying, fighting for rebounds,
hook shots, lay ups,
Immortality's boys with
no fears, no hang ups,
only the next basket
and playing away
the next hormone surge.

We cleared our pimples
and felt like men,
tall for our age—
same birthday,
Corsican Brothers of Queens,
high stool sitters
at the Five Spot Café
listening to Monk,
faking our age,
sipping beer at the bar,
inhaling our smoke
while hiding our coughs.

Then to college,
medicine, law
careers,
no time for hoops,
no time for fun,
only hopes, dreams.

We married, had families,
settled, grew, lived
a highway apart, still close.
You became my patient.
For 23 years your ECG
defined you differently.
I saw your sternum split
and new blood routes created
for your starving heart.
Mortality is now with us,
worn on our shoulders
each day, each night.

Then so suddenly
no longer young
we each faced
different challenges,
tried to meet them
like fast breaks
on the playground court.
But challenges are met
for only so long—
you slumped at your desk
and you were gone
long before the sirens
reached Bellevue's door.

Now your ashes
mix with Rockaway's sand,
grey specks on a white canvas.
I said *Kaddish* for you
for thirty days.
You wouldn't have wanted that
but what is a brother to do?
When I visit my parents' graves
I will stop at our beach
and watch the waves,
looking for grey specks
glistening on white sand.
Perhaps then I will believe
what still seems unreal
for one of Immorality's boys.

BRIT MILAH

For Solomon Zaret

At a round table
covered with white cloth,
topped by soft pillow,
I prepare for honored duty
in the ancient ritual:
naming my grandson
forever as a Jew.
I've been here before,
yet each trip
leaves my body limp.
I sit at the table,
tallit wrapped,
summoning images
that link generations
seen and never seen:
the slain family,
hanging limply from
snow-covered trees
in Russian winter woods,
the murdered grandfather
for whom I'm named,
my always loving father
whose eyes lit the night
when speaking of his grandsons.

The baby is placed on the pillow,
vulnerably secure,
surrounded by love
and anticipation.

My restraining hands lie lightly
on his small, fragile thighs.
He sleeps oblivious
to what will follow,
senses dulled by sweet wine.
The sharp blade's
swift movement,
steeped in millennia of experience,
is performed to perfection.
Only a soft whimper
from his tender mouth.
I return him to my son.
The small party begins.

Sleep well my grandson.
Now you've joined
the rest of us.
Wear your name proudly
without fear of predators.
No need to seek safety
in cold winter woods.

Sleep well my forebears.
Your sacrifices done,
your names, our name,
live in new worlds
propelled by memories
not to be forgotten.

INVITING LEONARD COHEN
TO OUR SUKKAH

Dear Leonard,

You're invited to our *sukkah*.
I know you're touring again.
If you're on the East Coast, please come.
Surely you remember *Sukkot*
from your Montreal youth.
Our people's time of joy,
a welcome relief after
Yom Kippur's solemnity.
A week of celebration
mixed with the transience
of hand-built fragile huts
and harvest spirituality.
We'll view the stars through
the thatched sukkah roof,
properly greet our forefather's spirits,
and you, the night's spiritual guest,
will mingle with Abraham and Isaac.
We'll talk, eat, drink, and sing.
Fall New England nights can be chilly.
Bring a sweater.

I missed your peak
when we both were young.
You grew famous
while I raised a family
and chased academic gold.
I've come late to your music,

but it's now with me daily,
on the treadmill,
walking hospital halls,
sitting in the hot tub.
Your "Anthem" metaphor gave
my dying patient hope;
she lived six more months.
There's much to discuss:
Moses and Buddha,
"Suzanne," "Famous
Blue Raincoat,"
when you stood
in synagogue and heard
Yom Kippur's "Who by Fire"
or chanted "Hallelujah."
We'll be discreet,
no other guests.
You choose the subjects,
I'm only suggesting.
It's our people's time of joy.
Let's be joyous together.
Do come if you can.

Sincerely,
B. Zaret

JOURNEYS

*The children of Israel journeyed from
Ramses and camped in Succoth. They
journeyed from Succoth and camped in
Etham...* – Numbers 33:1-49

*"The Torah enumerates the 42 encamp-
ments in the journeys of the children of
Israel who came out of Egypt. Each and
every one of us goes through our personal
42 journeys in life..."* –Baal Shem Tov

I journeyed from infancy
and camped in childhood.
It was not good dwelling there.
An only child's isolation,
days filled with poor health,
asthma's wheezes, allergies,
trips to doctors' offices.
Overweight and inactive,
loved intensely, but wrapped
in a stifling cloak
of overprotection.
Alone too often with
only thoughts and fears.
Lonely days, lonely nights.

I journeyed from childhood
and camped in adolescence.
Brooklyn's gray streets
replaced by Rockaway's
clean salt air,
breathing deeply without wheezing.
Crossing the

moat of isolation to
a world of new friends,
playground basketball,
hormone surges, first girlfriends,
new books and ideas.
Illness traded for health,
obesity for trimness.
No more extra wide pants,
no more doctors' visits.
Feeling new yearnings.
New fantasies filling dreams.
Old boundaries falling.
Tasting first independence
and savoring the flavor.
Growth had occurred.

I journeyed from adolescence
and camped in the land of college.
I liked dwelling there.
Learning now more than grades.
Facts meant something
of how life was lived.
Concepts, new worlds of art,
music, science, philosophy,
new friends, folk concerts
civil rights, beat poets,
the mind's fervor.
No matter that
days and nights
were filled with study,
labs, commuting on the Van Wyck.
I would do well,
I would be a doctor,

I would find love,
I would meet my life companion.
I had left my mind's *shtetl*
with intact wits
and a one way ticket.

I journeyed from the land of college
and camped in medical school,
a more intense process.
Endless facts,
memorization,
mnemonics to help.
Learning of life
by dissecting the dead.
Then, seeing live patients,
learning the art.
It was right; it fit.
After one year we married;
one room became home,
a sofa bed opened nightly.
With my life's work,
my life's partner,
right choices made,
new happiness found.
This was a good place to dwell.

I journeyed from medical school
and camped in medical training.
Internship yielded to residency,
residency to fellowship,
New York to Baltimore.
Days and nights were one;
acceptance of fatigue

now unacceptable,
carrying it on my shoulders
like a solder's pack.
Little sleep, little rest.
With each sleepless night
came more faith
in new skills,
more security.
Now doctor, internist,
then cardiologist,
a fellow learning
the joy of research.
Academics would be my life.
Two sons born;
my heart grew with each.
Medicine learned to share.
There were enough hours.
Across the ocean
guns roared in Vietnam.
TV's news counted
bodies with actuarial precision.
Protests, riots, sit-ins,
heroes falling to assassins.
New deeper fear,
awaiting news of
draft board decision;
anonymous executioners
would declare my next journey.
Hoping for strength and courage,
not able to stop trembling.

I journeyed from medical training
and camped in the military.
Two California years

far from Asia rice paddies.
Major, doctor,
Air Force cardiologist,
large hospital,
illness arriving on jet planes.
A time for patients;
surprisingly
a time for more research.
An opportunity to shed
East Coast provinciality.
The country bled,
Asia bled.
Then peace.

I journeyed from the military
and camped in academia.
Dwelling has been good,
the same camp ever since.
East Coast again,
Ivy League professor, doctor,
researcher, teacher, editor, leader.
Dreams fulfilled.
Also very much husband,
father, son, member of
a spiritual community.
In the first year
a third son born,
our family completed.
Full days, full nights,
uncertainty, chances,
lectures, travel, tenure.
Many threads in a tapestry
woven and rewoven.
We enjoyed, we pained,

we loved, we mourned,
we buried our parents.
Children journeyed to adulthood,
married and gave grandchildren
of immeasurable joy.
The encampment grew
to a second home
in the mountains,
doctoring and teaching in one,
painting and writing in the other.
Growing with decades,
very different people
from those who
crossed the country
in search of a
first permanent home,
first permanent job.
Illness now lives around us,
many funerals, many memorials.
The circle of friends narrows.

Surely there will be other journeys;
it's not clear how many.
But bags remain unpacked,
as I await each day,
hoping for strength and courage.

2008

FOR YOEL PEARL

Yoel, I phoned Myrna on Sunday,
she in Connecticut, I in Buenos Aires.
She told me of your death,
sudden, unexpected, final,
six weeks before your first visit to America.
After the call
I walked the foreign streets
of this foreign city.
My tears did not blind me
to young couples lying on park grass,
locked in embraces,
whispering Spanish words of love.
That day a scene which normally brought a smile
brought only sadness.
We were to show you
the New Haven Green, my University,
the Berkshires in summer.
A small artery to your big heart
did what no Arab bullet in two wars
could accomplish.
Now you lie on a *Tsvat* hill
beside generations of Pearls and kaballists,
a simple grave to be followed
in thirty days by a simple stone.

Our Israel visits no longer
will find me engulfed in your embrace,
pressed to your massive chest,
smothered by your broad arms—
you the *Hermon,*
my 185 pounds a mere foothill.

I will not hear your deep voice
singing a river of songs
as we traverse the Golan in your jeep
on uncharted army roads,
past barbed wire and old mine fields.
You loved every *dunam*.
You were Israel itself,
strong, fierce if need be,
beneath strength soft and warm.

We talked about your heart many times.
You tried to suppress
satiety, cigars,
but never quite succeeded.
The cardiologist stood impotent,
always in fear of today's news.

Tsvat's doors now will not be as blue.
The Golan will not shimmer at midday.
The *Kinneret* will not reflect its sunsets
in pastels my canvas seeks to capture.
Tel Aviv's rhythm will be slower.
Jerusalem will be less spiritual.

We will place pebbles on your stone
and chant *Kaddish,* my tears
will wet dry soil by your grave.
Yoel, I couldn't get you to listen.
You gambled, we all lost.
I will try to honor your life by other deeds.
May your memory be a blessing.

FOR PRIMO LEVI

I know you
only through words,
in translation.
Snow is toes frozen,
sun is mouth burning,
life is
hunger, fear,
pain, survival,
hope.

Far from Dante
in Auschwitz,
far from warm rooms,
burning ideas,
youth's spirit;
far from mountain hikes,
clear air,
open vistas.
An old life
once young,
in translation.

Akiba said
everything is foreseen,
yet freedom of choice
is granted.
Did you believe that
in Buna's long night?

Everything is foreseen.
The will to live—

is it stronger?
They say,
years later,
in gravity's last seconds
you lost that will.
Does it matter?

I cherish you
through words.
They make me strong
and make me cry.
I see them
at home
and on the road,
morning and night.
They bind me
to you,
in translation.

A WALK IN TAORMINA

Corso Umberto.
Cobblestones for tourist feet.
Shop windows,
Sicily's wares:
linen,
ceramics,
souvenirs.
Belle, bonne, schon
Taormina,
eagle-high.
Below, sea;
above, castle.
Old amphitheater,
Greek echoes.
Distant Etna
ever on guard,
protecting
with Cyrano's plume
and quiet anger.
A good place for
tourist eyes,
tourist feet.

A chorus of
pizza shops
linking hands
along the *via*
singing of their fate.
Each different, each the same.
A street corner—
Via del Ghetto,

no more.
A street sign,
no plaque, no story.
(Do only my eyes see this?)
Winding furtively,
a maze only it knows.
Little alleys,
cold scarred stone.

Touch yields no
vibration.
Balcony bougainvillea
do not brighten.
No *mazuzot,*
no noise,
no song.
Scarred stone
and anguish.

Here once
young boys of Friday
raced to greet
the Sabbath Queen.
"Lecha dodi, likrat kallah."
Heders buzzed
with life and learning.
Families grew, generations passed.
Every year
Tisha B'Av laments
filled the alleys—
"Alas, lonely sits the city
once great with people."
They were
told to leave—

1492.
No return ticket.
One remnant,
a street sign.

The sun brightens,
tourists smile on
the next street,
Via Garibaldi.
Guides nod
and explain.
Not like
Via del Ghetto.

TEACH ME

In honor of Rabbi Richard Eisenberg's
tenure at Congregation B'nai Jacob
(1994-2007)

Teach me
to open old doors
to new places
and new doors
to old questions.
Teach me
to be a tree
with few branches
but many roots,
unmoved by the wind.
Teach me to be a rabbi.

Teach me
to comfort
each time
I stand before
a hole in the earth,
soon to be filled.
Teach me
to rejoice
each time
I stand beneath the canopy
joining two souls.
Teach me to be a rabbi.

Teach me
to always answer,

whatever time,
though my body aches
and my head is full.
Teach me to soothe those
whom time has forgotten
and to be patient with
those who forget
the long time before them.
Teach me to be a rabbi.

Teach me
to remember
the day is short,
the task is great.
Teach me to follow the straight path,
not to fear
the surrounding woods.
Teach me
not to ignore
a new light,
inside or out,
heralding
a new future.
and if I follow,
above all,
teach me always to be a rabbi.

III. Doctoring

EPIPHANY

Over forty years ago,
an intern only three months,
he faced early morning
with sleep-denied eyes
from red brick Bellevue's
highest window.
The night had been spent
wrestling death's angel.
He'd won this time.
Saving a life
if only for a night
took his tired mind
to heights never
learned in school.
With emptied coffee cup,
he watched an October sun
rise over the East River.
Purple, pink and orange
cast the sky in fire's colors.
Clouds burned bush-red.
The burning sky spoke
in clear voice:
he had overcome
novice doubts and fears;
medicine was his life's road.
In that moment
his name changed forever.

With deep breath and deeper smile
he hurried to the on-call room.

Enough time to brush teeth,
shave, change a shirt.
Then with quickened step
and straightened shoulders
he bounded up the stairs,
ready for morning rounds.

THE JEWISH HOME
FOR THE AGED

For B.H.

Stride up the incline
toward the patient wing,
a windowless hallway
with institutional green walls
knowing neither sun nor shade:
an ascent into decline.
Pass the wall of memorial boards,
covered with brass plaques,
marking residents
who ended life here
(as if a reminder is necessary).
Then under the ceiling
that leaks in heavy rains.
Next the courtyard
where some sit
in wheelchairs, still
enjoying their cigarettes.
Finally the wing's double doors,
guarding entry and exit.

Since my patient transferred
I come here often.
I've cared for her over twenty years.
I doubt we'll make twenty-one.
My feet know the way without me.
The staff greet me; I'm a regular.
Decay is pervasive

in both the drab walls
and those within them.
Odors of dried urine
and body lotion blend.
The two dance together
just below the ceiling,
an olfactory canopy
of despair and resignation.
Medicine now does little
for my patient's frail
ninety-two-year body.
Infirmity succumbs to infirmity,
yet her mind remains firm.
Poetry, photos and stories
replace new pills and procedures.
They work for short periods,
bring smiles to her thin, saddened face.
I will continue these visits
despite their pain.
Abandonment is not an option.
On the final part of our journey
caring has replaced healing,
soothing has replaced science.

FORTY-TWO YEARS

Forty-two years I've been called *doctor*.
Six letters defining me
as much as *husband, father, son*.
First as new intern,
so eager, so fearful,
dressed in white pants and jacket
stiff with yesterday's starch.
Now professor's name
is stitched on my soft white lab coat
draped on stooping shoulders
as I stride the boundaries
of my hospital domain.
I've cared for patients in the same clinic
for more than three decades.
Some have been with me almost as long.
Many have now grown frail,
others are no longer here.
We age together.
I wear them around my neck
like a long string of pearls,
each self-contained,
a lesson of illness, healing or death.
Each a reminder
of a privileged state,
my six letter name.
They've kept me whole over
decades in the lab and at the desk.
I still pain when they fail
and feel the rush of intern's joy
when they recover.

A bit surprising after forty-two years.
If ever the feelings cease
I'll nestle my stethoscope
in the desk's lower drawer
and with some remorse
begin reading the many books
that have been waiting a lifetime for me.

YOU'RE MY DOCTOR

A car stopped suddenly
on Howard Avenue
allowing me to cross
from garage to office
with head down, unimpeded.
Once on the other street side
I waved.
As he passed, the driver
yelled "You're my doctor."
His speed was too fast
for me to see his face.

All I could do
was smile
and nod my head.

Perhaps some time soon
when visiting my office
he'll reveal himself.
Then I'll offer thanks properly
and tell him
a simple one-second
acknowledgement
was all the fee needed
for years to come.

HOLDING HANDS

Every day the medical center
fills my eyes
with profiles of disease
long before I arrive
at my patients' hospital rooms.
I see couples
walking hand in hand
across trafficked streets
from garage to hospital,
navigating the medical center
down serpiginous hallways,
searching for unmarked offices.
They are many
years past teen romance,
hands now linked to form
new life lines.

PROFESSORS OF FACADE

I suspect every university
has its Professors of Facade
who devote great strength
and market skills
to sculpting an image
of merit without deed.
No doubt bright,
always overachieving,
they worship Facade,
wrapping themselves in it
like morning *tefellin*.
Some disguise in
well pressed suits and
matching color ties,
others in ripped sweaters
and old blue jeans.
Some mutter, some orate,
emphasizing the weight
of each unimportant word.
Some motor in well-
polished convertibles,
others cycle to work
on shabby Schwinns.
Whatever the guise,
Professors of Facade
somehow deceive
most around them.
As with beggars and thieves,
God loves Professors of Facade.

CHRONOLOGY

"Do me a favor,"
my colleague said—
"I'd like a tube of blood.
I'm studying lymphocytes
in young and old men.
You're over 65?"
"Yes, but I'm still quite young,"
I replied,
trying to hide
an anxious annoyance.
I exercise every day,
I lift weights,
I split firewood.
On rounds
I lead my trainees
to hospital staircases.
I doctor, teach, write and paint.
I'm not old.

"You're over 65,"
he said again—
"you could be in my study."
Very cold,
very scientific,
very accurate.

I tell my older patients
not merely to count years.
Physiology trumps chronology,
I say.

But chronology wins
when a colleague asks for a tube
of my over-65 blood.
No matter
the endless treadmill hours,
I've now joined
a new cohort,
meeting rigid criteria.
Surely I'll receive
other requests.
Next time
there'll be no angst.
I'll offer my blood
willingly, then retreat
to the nearest staircase.

IV. IN THE LAND OF CANCER

MAN PLANS AND GOD LAUGHS

"Man plans and God laughs,"
my father, a *shtetl* existentialist,
told me hundreds of times
in a charming Yiddish
imbued with wisdom
learned in life, not books.
I had to wait till college
and Camus and Sartre
to understand what he learned
as a young teenager.
"Man plans and God laughs."
Myrna and I had calculated our future
with anticipated precision.
Then celestial laughter
erased the blueprints,
canceled the trips,
removed the many joys
we thought awaited us.
We live in the Land of Cancer,
a surreal place
filled with plans and no plans,
dreams and no dreams,
hope and no hope,
reality and no reality.
I try not to plan now;
so I hear no laughter,
only the beating
of an inner heart,
a clock that seeks
to push time backward,
reliving fifty years together.

GOD OF CANCER

God of cancer,
you are an evil tease.
You give us scattered
hours, even days
of happiness and ease.
Then you take it all back
replaced with weakness, pain,
sleeplessness, fear.
God of cancer,
you are a relentless foe,
one I cannot defeat
no matter my plan.
If you were a man
I would grasp your throat
and squeeze with every
ounce of my strength
until your face blued
and your breath ceased.
I would stand over
your lifeless body
with arms raised
despite my oath to heal.
But you are not a man
and I am not a god.
Let us continue the struggle.
I will not concede,
even as you make the rules,
you evil tease, you relentless foe.

PILL COUNT

It started in winter
when chemo weakened her
as never before.
Morning and evening
I began counting pills,
preparing her medications,
both those that eased and
those that damaged.
Readying each pill
was my act of love.
Now in summer
I continue the routine,
although she is often stronger,
capable of doing this herself.
In the Land of Cancer
the multicolored pills
provide a palette
for new art,
at the same time
concrete and abstract.
I welcome the task:
treatment yields hope,
even if illusory.
May the ritual continue
like all the other
survival methods
linking us together
as we cope, day by day,
in the Land of Cancer.

STOP AND SHOP

The aisles of the Stop and Shop
are now as familiar
as the halls of my medical center.
Market staff are known to me,
and my face to them,
more than interns in the CCU.
They greet me
as I stumble through my weekly trek.
Thursday is shopping day—
I come armed with her list,
carefully constructed to
aid my navigation past
cold cereal, coffee, canned goods.
I carry an envelope
filled with clipped coupons
to be redeemed at the register.
When I hand them to the clerk
I always add that this
is my wife's thing, not mine.
Coupons embarrass me,
offending my professorial persona.

It upsets her that she's
usually too weak to do the shopping.
It was part of her biorhythm.
I can never equal her precision
or pantry organization;
I am her arms and legs.
She makes the list, I follow.
I walk the aisles of Stop and Shop,

clean, do laundry,
make beds, cook, and drive.

If I ever forget
let my right hand wither,
let my tongue no longer speak.

TORAH READING
IN THE LAND OF CANCER

The Torah words dance off her lips
with effortless grace—
Degas ballerinas,
they move, spin, leap
above the heads of
the seated congregants,
surrounding all in the radiance
of ancient story, deeds, laws.
Ears hear perfect Hebrew reading,
as they have for decades.
But eyes now see a body
ravaged by disease
and its treatment.

For her 17 months
in the Land of Cancer
she has continued to read Torah
with uncommon precision,
unwilling to yield,
withstanding all physical assaults,
not asking for sympathy,
rising from fatigue's bed
to meet her joyous *Shabbat* task.
Her aura and skill
in the face of unrelenting illness
always inspire those listening.
They marvel at her courage, dignity,
elegance under siege.
Her reading gives them strength,

while Torah words strengthen her.
Afterward she remains ebullient
well into the afternoon.
By evening the rush is gone,
Torah endorphins dissipated.

I no longer suggest she read Torah less often.
Time has proven me wrong.
She continues on, ignoring
disease, pain, fatigue:
a true woman of valor.
Let her readings continue to sustain
as the words dance off her lips.

MOMENTS OF REPRIEVE

Sometime soon
(who knows how long)
I will wake
and she will not be there.
I will turn to an empty place
still with pillow but
filled with life's absence.
But this spring morning
I awaken as she touches me.
For a few minutes
there is no future, no pain,
no weekly treatment,
no cancer destroying her bones.
Only two people
lost in each other
with welcomed warmth and quiet passion.
Brief moments of reprieve
in the Land of Cancer.

IN THE LAND OF CANCER

Since moving to
the Land of Cancer
each day is a ride
on my seesaw
of hope and reality.
When she has a good scan
I elevate skyward.
If her scan worsens
or treatment yields
fearful side effects,
I fall rapidly,
jarred by the impact
of landing on the hard ground:
new chemo,
more radiation,
new issues—
nights of nausea,
days of fatigue.

As a young boy on a
blacktop Brooklyn playground
I once rode a seesaw,
my urban birch tree.
I longed for the jolting ride in space,
the escape from life's routines,
eagerly waiting for the hard bounce
as ground was touched again.

The rides now differ:
I avoid going too high—
the fall should be softer.
Above all, the ride should continue.
Fifteen months in the Land of Cancer.

SHALOM ALEICHEM
IN THE LAND OF CANCER

Welcome angels—
we wish you peace
even if peace escapes us
and fear engulfs us.

Come to us in peace
even when cancer eats
at her bones
and steals her strength.

Bless us with peace
even as disease and
treatment each
extracts its toll.

Leave us in peace
even if this Shabbat
may be as painful
as the last, or next to last
or one to follow.

THE LAST HOURS

In the last hours
secretions filled your airways.
You breathed in strained noisy tones,
announcing death's imminence.
We had agreed you'd stay at home;
I fed narcotics
in liquid drops
since you no longer
could swallow pills.
Turning you on your side
made breathing easier.
I talked to you
in a soft voice:
places and events
that forged a
wonderful life together,
our children,
our grandchildren.
Whether you heard or not,
I continued.
We both knew
on separate levels
that this was our
last night together.
I lit *Chanukah* candles
and sang the prayers.
I believed you were aware.
Tonight the miracle of burning oil
would bring no new miracles.
Tomorrow would bring funeral plans.

Your eulogy, obituary
already written,
I was ready for this moment
as you were,
the last atom of resistance
drained from your wasted body.
Your breathing first slowed
then finally stopped.
For the first time in months
your face was peaceful.
Serenity replaced suffering,
dignity replaced defeat.
I closed your eye lids,
kissed your cold forehead
then waited for the Hospice nurse
to come and
pronounce you dead.
Now call the kids,
the funeral director,
a few friends.
Make ready for all
I had dreaded over
the past twenty months.

V. AND BEYOND

WALLTALK

When the god of cancer
took you for himself
and *Shivah* ended,
our life's home,
void of companionship,
was engulfed in the cold
cloak of loneliness,
time filled by TV sports,
crossword puzzles,
mindless magazines.
Then, as with survivors before me,
walltalk filled the void.
Walltalk:
words spoken
with responses
reverberating back
sonar-like—
fears voiced,
needs expressed,
questions asked,
blame dispensed,
problems solved,
frustrations laid bare.
The companion walls
never ignore,
attentive to each issue,
silently helping the
questioner answer himself.
Sometimes walltalk
is interrupted by tears.
Then dialogue ends.

YESTERDAY'S SOUP POT

Now you've left me.
The god of cancer
has claimed his due.
No matter how intense the fight,
the outcome was assured long ago.
Now you've left me.
The emptiness overwhelms.
The void descends
deeper than can be fathomed—
when sleep should come,
when life should prevail,
when work should be done,
when pleasure should arrive.

It is the uncleaned pot,
in which I cooked yesterday's soup,
now emptied, but still lined
with caked residue
of last night's treat.
A memory of pleasant tastes.
But memories can't replace
satisfying smells,
soup touching my palate,
sliding smoothly
past my mouth,
filling my waiting stomach,
warming my innards,
protecting from the cold.

PAPER PLATE PESACH

For the first time
I face *Pesach* without you,
my holiday music
now deeply atonal.
The two weeks before
are eerily unfrenzied.
Ovens, refrigerators
remain untended,
neither they nor I
spiritually cleansed.
No cleaning or scrubbing,
no body aches or fatigue.
No transport of
endless cartons filled with
plates, pans, utensils.
This *Pesach* is
different from all others.
Our home, once
ritual's bastion,
this year
paralyzed,
without your gravity
no longer holiday's sun
around which family orbits.
Seders will be elsewhere,
with children or friends.
It is my holiday
of wandering avoidance.
In the few nights at home
paper plates and plastic
forks will suffice.

This is our time of freedom
to be remembered, relived.
This year, I, memory's slave,
will traverse different waters.
While still afflicted,
I eat affliction's bread
on white paper plates,
fleeing from loneliness,
while striving
for new hope, new freedom.

ON THE GARDEN STATE PARKWAY

Clear morning in December,
unseasonably warm;
solar exclamations
punctuate the cloudless sky.
Driving south
the car moves with
serene speed.
Springsteen blares
on the radio:
"...can't start a fire
without a spark..."
My head bobs with the beat.
No need for sparks;
my fire has burned
white hot for hours.
The untrafficked parkway,
the sunlight,
the feeling of ease,
the music,
all coalesce
to provide
unparalleled joy.
I move leftward
to pass a slow moving
black vehicle.

When alongside
I see that
it is a hearse,
emptied of contents,
ready to start a new day
with new passengers.
While sun shines above
and euphoria blooms below
the hearse issues
its proclamation.
In that moment
Springstein succumbs to Sisyphus.

Kohelet teaches that
there are times for everything,
even abrupt return
to harsh reality
when all seems ideal
until you pass
a slow moving hearse
traveling in the right lane.

CHERISH THE MEMORIES

Cherish the memories
but also cherish the future.
I tell myself this
when awakening
long before the sky lightens,
still craving sleep denied;
when my feet touch
the treadmill and my
arms lift weights;
when forcing myself
to eat, though not hungry.

Days follow days,
each filled with duties, escape.
But in evening
I return
to the dark house of winter,
to a future,
so fearsome, so new.

BLESSED IS THE SCAR

Blessed is the scar
that time allows
to grow where
once a deep wound
extended under
opened skin and
jagged edges
into torn muscle.
Blessed is the scar
continuing
tender to touch.
Blessed is the scar
that is the force
of returning function,
restoring strength
to reenter life.

FOR RENÉE

First, small blue patches
dot the cloud tapestry,
then wider swathes,
finally, a bright cloudless sky.
Winter's siege has passed.

A DOOR OPENS

A door, once ajar, opens
unexpectedly.
No warning, no hint.
A new threshold exposed,
faced at first
tentatively, fearfully.
The pace increases.
Yesterday's first steps
quicken...

A CHAGALL CANVAS

The Audi travels south
with zest and anticipation,
speed limit far in
my rear view mirror,
Connecticut miles behind.
Chagall-like,
two figures hover above the car,
embracing as they float,
glittering in the early morning sun.
They bear our likeness,
imbued with brightness
of blues, reds and violets,
today's Marc and Bella.
But below them no Paris,
no Eiffel Tower or cobblestone streets,
no *shtetls* or fiddlers;
only billboards and shopping centers
along the Jersey highway.
The couple remains aloft
throughout the drive,
guiding and protecting.
The road
is a highway of gold
ending in a new Paris
where a new Bella waits,
making me whole once again.

ARE YOU DATING YET?

"Are you dating yet?"
she asked casually.
"It's time, you know."
At the bat mitzvah table
the unexpected words,
uttered with no prelude
left my jaw slack,
my limbs limp.
The party had already
touched many triggers,
awakenings of times past
darkening celebration's joy.
Why this inquiry?
Was it caring,
idle conversation,
inquisitiveness,
or something more?
She couldn't have known
that two days before
an anniversary marking
forty-eight years together
had occurred in silence
at a secluded grave site.
Perhaps experience
never taught her
that words can open wounds
meant to heal,
and singe the heart.

JOURNEYS II

This *Shabbat,* eight months without you,
the Book of Numbers recounts
the journeys in the wilderness.
Your chanting of this portion,
one of my favorites, was rhapsodic.
The lilting journey trope
spilled sweetly from your lips,
honeyed drops from history's jar.
I'm honored with the second *aliyah.*
My eyes and ears encounter
our tribes' campsites and travels.
Leaning over the Torah scroll
I am transported to times
before your cancer.
I hear your voice;
I see your *yad* move
gracefully across the text.
During the last *aliyah*
a baby receives her Hebrew name,
Malka, the same as yours.
I am moved by the beauty
of life's symmetry.
For the first time
memory triggers
neither pain nor tears.

How welcome this healing day
that readies for new journeys.
You will always travel with me,
deeply nurtured within.

But now as I tread
I will no longer stoop
under the past's heavy load.
Today I start a new journey,
with straight posture,
my face aglow
with the smile of passage.

HURRICANE IRENE

For days they prepared us:
hourly computer models
tracked the storm's path.
Weathermen feasted on
their projections
like gourmet dinners.
Myrna's unveiling,
long ago set for storm day,
is put off three weeks.

Finally wind and rain arrive,
pounding all in their path.
Denied power and water,
I walk through my home,
for years too large for two.
I am oppressed
by a weighty cloak of darkness
and isolation.
Our large living room,
once alit with the joy
of family seders,
now sits in black,
more *Tisha B'Av* than *Pesach*.
Yahrzeit candles,
strategically placed,
furnish modest light.
Can these candles
bought to memorialize
my father, my mother, my wife
also illuminate rooms?

In this lonely of lonelies
thoughts are confronted
in stifling quiet,
the vice of darkness.
My flashlight leads
through the black house
and to basement inspections
until fatigue causes
sleep to come, grudgingly.

Power returns in two days,
ahead of all predictions.
And there is light from darkness,
and there is water from dry taps,
and there is the world
seen with fresh eyes.
And there is jubilation.
I stride with manic vigor
from room to room and
to my still dry basement.

I have faced the
lonely of lonelies.
It's time to move on.

UNVEILING

We gather by the gravesite
at cemetery's edge.
Psalms, readings, *El Malei,*
reminiscences, *Kaddish,*
all uttered with
tears and pain,
only partially softened
by nine months' passage.
The covering is removed.
This veil hides
no bride's face.
Before me white granite,
unsmiling, immovable,
fixed forever in space and time,
carved with nine words
to distill a life's essence:
BELOVED WIFE,
MOTHER, GRANDMOTHER,
INSPIRING TORAH READER,
TEACHER, SCHOLAR.
Each word a *shofar* sound;
notes soon to be heard
in the days ahead,
heralding a New Year
of renewed prayer,
renewed repentance,
renewed hope.
A New Year
and a new roster
of who will live,
who will die,
who by fire,
who by water,
who by cancer...

SNOW IN OCTOBER

Heavy snow in October:
how odd,
with *Sukkot*
recently ended
and autumn colors
not fully manifest.
Limbs of still
green-leafed trees
crack and fall
under snow's weight.
Power losses abound,
whole towns paralyzed.
I stand awed
by nature's deadly game,
thankful to be spared
at least for now.
This is New England,
not the Rockies.
Snow never
falls in October.
Too much
to comprehend
after recent hurricane
and floods.
Odd occurrences
suited for odd times.

But the unusual
no longer surprises.
As we warm globally

the unexpected has
become routine;
former losers
now winners.
Did life not balance
my recent grief,
charting a new course
to navigate the
white waters of
these odd times?

THIS WINTER'S POND

Last night's rain
melted the pond's
first ice covering.
I awaken to
hemlock and cloud
reflections,
a winter rarity.
Soon the morning's
late December chill
again induces
water to freeze
and reflections to vanish.
New light snow
whitens the fresh ice
and sugars the shore
with tasty frosting,
while winds gently
coerce laurel
and hemlock
into graceful movement.
No car noise
or children's shouts
across the pond,
only the sounds of
pencil on paper
and peaceful breathing.
As I look from my desk
the cold landscape
warms my eyes
and invites me to enter.

Am I the only person
living this moment?
Solitude's quiet,
once my oven
for reheating memories,
no longer causes sorrow.
I have regained
my Berkshire haven,
last year's loneliness
today's serenity.

THE TREE AND THE VINE

When walking
my long driveway
I often pause to
view a special tree
and the leafy vine
encircling the trunk as
it spirals skyward.
From afar they are as one.
But up close there
are separate roots.
The tree stands
with sturdiness
endowed by decades of growth.
The vine, a newcomer,
thin yet robust,
ascends serpiginously
with DNA grace.
In spring the two
bloom side by side.
In autumn their
leaves turn gold
together as if
responding to a common cue.
Throughout the year
they remain
wrapped in embrace.
Much like future and past,
they've learned the secret
of living together.

VI. BERKSHIRES

SNOW DANCE

Last night's snow
covers woods
and frozen pond
like a freshly made bed.
Hemlock boughs
laden by snow's weight
bend supplely,
arch downward and interlace.
Are they burdened
or just resting,
waiting for a wind gust
to initiate their
undulating dance?
When that movement comes,
slowly and gracefully
they release their snow—
oriental dancers
shedding their veils.
Free of added weight
boughs leap skyward.
The ballet concludes.

In the morning blueness
the air is still.
Cold stings my cheeks
and burns my fingers.
But my eyes
scan the floor
seeking the ideal hemlock
to partner
in the next dance.

RHODODENDRONS
IN WINTER

The rhododendrons
outside my winter window
are forlorn.
Their plump summer leaves
are shriveled,
pointing downward.
I'd like to plod
through the snow,
warm them, tell them
not to despair.
They should know
I restlessly await
their violet, purple and pink.
Together we will
smile into spring,
stretch our stiff limbs,
and once again
renew ourselves.

WHEN THE SLEET STOPPED

The sleet has stopped.
We want a winter night hour
in the tub.
I'll shovel a path on the deck.
The cold will shock to start,
but swirling warm water
will cover to our chins.
Let's go now.
Dinner can wait.
Leave the phone inside.
Like snow on our deck
time can freeze.
We wanted an hour.
Now it's ours.

The Bard said
man has seven ages.
I think there are more.
He never delighted in
a winter Berkshire night
when the sleet has stopped,
or walked a new path
to warm swirling water
when, despite
grey hair and creaky joints,
we dance into the darkness
and all that follows.

SNOW COTTON

Winter Berkshire snow
covers
everything I see
quietly.
Tree branches,
ground lights,
stone fountain,
wood pile
all sleep
beneath tufts of cotton
softly.
I love
snow cotton,
itself an art form,
yet still conforming
to what's beneath,
reminding me
what Spring will show.

My mother always dabbed
my childhood bruises
with tufts of cotton
dipped in peroxide.
I sat in the chair
obediently
as she soothed
wound and ego
with uncommon
love and tenderness.
There was burning,
as the peroxide welled up

like high tide ocean foam,
cotton white over wound red.
Brown iodine soon followed
and the painted shin
was again ready to play.
I mostly remember
the peroxide sting,
when I closed my eyes
and clenched my jaw
fearfully.
The relief that followed
is lost to time.

Now cold winter Sundays find
Berkshire snow cotton
piled high,
awakening and soothing.
Each tuft provides relief.
But this time,
no burning.

CHANGE OF SEASONS

It's time to trade
snow shovel and ice chipper
for rake and axe.
Painting in gradations of white
has grown tiresome.
Tubes of yellow, green and red paint
long to respond, explode
onto palate and landscape canvas,
like late winter buds
bursting into spring.

My friends in warmer climes
never have this end-of-March feeling.
They tread boringly into spring.
I prefer my Berkshire seasons,
each a jewel,
but each with limits, borders.
When I'm ready to scream
"Not another winter day!"
somehow snow begins to melt,
buds explode on their branches,
yellow paint emerges from its tube.

I await each sequence
of farewell and welcome,
always repeating, yet always fresh.
Pity those in warmer climes
who pass seasons by only
changing into different swim suits.

WOODPILE AFTER WINTER

My woodpile is sadly depleted.
Its covering tarp hangs loosely
over what few logs remain,
like old clothing
after a strenuous diet.
No longer under mounds of snow,
the sagging tarp accumulates
pockets of water after spring rain,
a breeding site for mosquitoes.
Worry not, my woodpile—
soon it will be fall.
The pond will echo the sound
of sledge hammer hitting wedge.
You will be returned to robustness,
standing proudly in the autumn sun,
making ready for winter's sacrifice.

FIRST KAYAK OF SUMMER

The paddle announces each stroke
upon entering still water,
followed by the sound
of a chorus of drops.
Beyond my paddle's voice
the pond is wrapped in quiet.
The well-rested kayak
glides forward into summer.
Despite the late hour
the sun still warms.
A manganese blue sky
is punctuated
by puffed clouds.
I want to reach down
and touch their reflections,
a child's game still gleefully played.
A beaver crosses my path
while returning to his lodge,
the solo welcome
for summer's first kayak.

Some travel to Delphi.
I find Delphi in mirror water.
I've waited a long winter
to return to my oracle,
again to meet my muses
who swim with beavers.

BERKSHIRE LIGHT

An hour before dusk
in a Berkshire summer!
Hemlock branches
glow in the western sun.
They turn yellow and orange
and their underbellies
shadow darkly.
Their dimensions deepen
with each minute.
In that hour I pray
sunset never comes.
I live in a Hopper world
of bold color
and contrast.
I want nothing more.

We sit in the tub
watching the trees change
while they watch us.
Below, the pond glistens.
The water reflects
a quiet sky
of pink and vermillion.

Above us
a cloud of insects hover,
always moving—

but only side to side.
They never come close.

Perhaps in this hour
they concede
we belong here too.

SCENT OF EARLY MORNING LOVE

As I leave our bed
wrapped in pleasing memory,
scent of early morning love is over me.
I inhale it lifting first coffee mug
to my lips. It lingers while driving
to Hall's for the morning paper
and later hovers
as I stand by the easel,
lost in color.
At noon the scent
propels my shovel deeply
into the small hill of mulch, soon
spread over garden beds.
By mid-afternoon the sweetness
has vaporized into Berkshire summer,
but only for the moment.
There will be more mornings,
followed by more scents.

I DON'T KNOW

No one is about,
not even geese.
I stand at the window,
coffee mug in hand.
The pond is all mine.
West shore trees reflect deeply;
their illuminated tops dance
boldly in air and water,
asking for more warmth.
And tomorrow?
I don't know.

Midday, at the easel
over three hours.
Colors come easily.
My brush darts across the canvas
like the shepherd's dog
tending its flock.
Stroke yields to stroke,
oils layer and blend,
palette knife mixes confidently.
And tomorrow's colors?
I don't know.

The afternoon is moving rocks,
splitting wood, raking leaves,
bonding with this land
I love so deeply.
Dusk follows.
Enough work.

Time for the hot tub,
dinner with red wine,
later lying in each other's arms.
No sound but delight.
Then sweet sleep.
And tomorrow?
I don't know, I don't know.

NOTES

Page 7, "My Father's Kosher Butcher Shop." *Shabbat* is Hebrew for the Sabbath.

Page 10, "For Lew Herman." *Kaddish* is the memorial prayer said several times a day for 1-11 months, depending upon the relationship of the mourner to the deceased.

Page 13, "Brit Milah." *Brit Milah* is the Hebrew term for ritual circumcism, often called *bris* in Yiddish, performed on the 8th day after birth. *Tallit* is a prayer shawl worn during prayers and rituals.

Page 15, "Inviting Leonard Cohen to Our Sukkah." A *sukkah* is a booth built to celebrate the festival of *Sukkot,* known as the Festival of Booths or Tabernacles. During the holiday, which lasts 8 days in the diaspora, meals are served in the sukkah. *Yom Kippur* is the Day of Atonement.

Page 17, "Journeys." Baal Shem Tov was an Eighteenth Century mystical rabbi who is considered the founder of Chassidism. *Shtetl* is Yiddish for a small town with a large Jewish population in Central and Eastern Europe. These towns were destroyed during the Holocaust.

Page 23 , "For Yoel Pearl." *Tsvat* is the Hebrew name of the Northern Israeli city of Safed. Mount Hermon is the highest mountain in the Golan Heights. *Dunam* is a measure of land used in the Ottoman Empire and still employed in the Middle East. A dunam is defined as 1,000 square meters. *Kinneret* is Hebrew for the sea of Galilee. *Kaddish:* see note for page 10.

Page 25, "For Primo Levi." Primo Levi was an Italian Jew and chemist who survived the Holocaust to become an internationally known writer. It is generally considered that he committed suicide, although this view has been challenged. Buna was the largest sub-camp of Auschwitz. It contained a factory where Levi worked as a chemist. Akiba was one of Judaism's great rabbinic scholars.

Page 28, "A Walk in Taormina." *Mazuzot* is the plural of the Hebrew *mezuzah,* a case containing parchment inscribed with verses from the Torah that is placed on the door frame of a Jewish home. *Lecha dodi* is a song that is chanted in synagogue on Friday evenings to greet the Sabbath. *Heder* is a Jewish school for young children. *Tisha B'Av* is the ninth day of the Hebrew month Av. This is a fast day that commemorates the destruction of both the first and second temples in Jerusalem as well as other tragedies that have befallen the Jewish people. "Alas, lonely sits the city…" is the opening phrase of Jeremiah's "Lamentations," which is chanted on Tisha B'Av.

Page 43, "Professors of Facade." *Tefellin* is Hebrew for *phylacteries,* which are small black leather boxes containing scrolls of parchment inscribed with verses from the Torah. The boxes are attached to leather straps which are wrapped around the arm and hand as well as being placed on the forehead. They are worn during weekday morning prayer.

Page 49, "Man Plans and God Laughs." *Shtetel:* see note for page 17.

Page 52, "Stop and Shop." *CCU* is the abbreviation for *Coronary Care Unit.*

Page 54, "Torah Reading in the Land of Cancer." The *Torah* comprises the 5 books of Moses. Portions are chanted from a parchment scroll on the Sabbath, on holidays, and on Monday and Thursday mornings. *Shabbat:* see page 7. *Endorphins* are endogenously produced opiates.

Page 59, "Shalom Aleichem In the Land of Cancer." *Shalom Aleichem* is a Hebrew term of greeting. In this instance it also refers to the traditional four-stanza song welcoming the Sabbath angels that is sung at the dinner table at the beginning of the Sabbath.

Page 60, "The Last Hours." *Chanukah* is the Jewish Festival of Lights during which candles are lit in increasing numbers for eight successive nights.

Page 65, "Walltalk." *Shivah* is the traditional seven-day mourning period.

Page 67, "Paper Plate Pesach." *Pesach* is Hebrew for Passover. *Seder* is the traditional family celebration occurring the first two nights of the Passover holiday. *Matzoh* is also referred to as the "bread of affliction."

Page 70, "On the Garden State Parkway." *Kohelet* is Hebrew for Ecclesiastes.

Page 75, "A Chagall Canvas." *Shtetl*: see note for p. 17.

Page 76, "Are You Dating Yet?" *Bat mitzvah* is the celebration of the rite of passage for a Jewish girl, comparable to *bar mitzvah* for a boy.

Page 77, "Journeys II." *Shabbat*: see note for p. 7. *Yad*, literally Hebrew for "hand," is a pointer, usually made of silver, used to point to the Torah text while a reader chants the selected portion. *Aliyah* is the honor of being called to the Torah during the morning reading.

Page 79, "Hurricane Irene." *Unveiling* is the ceremony at the grave site marking the removal of a cloth covering the newly placed headstone; it is performed during the year after death. *Tisha B'Av*: see note for page 28. *Yahrzeit* is the date in the Hebrew calendar marking the anniversary of a person's death. On that date a 24-hour memorial candle is lit. *Pesach:* see note for page 67. *Seder:* see note for page 67.

Page 81, "Unveiling." *Unveiling:* see note for page 79. *El Malei* are the first words of a memorial prayer. *Kaddish:* see note for page 10. *Shofar* is a ram's horn that is blown several times during the High Holy Days. "Who will live…" is a portion of a prayer recited during Yom Kippur.

Page 82, "Snow in October." *Sukkot:* see note for page 15.

About the Author

Dr. Barry L. Zaret's *Journeys* is his debut poetry collection. His poems have appeared in *Caduceus, Pharos,* and *Long River Run*. Several of his poems have been set to music and have been performed in concert. In his other life, Dr. Zaret is a cardiologist who has been on the faculty of Yale University School of Medicine since 1973. He served as Chief of Cardiology there and at Yale New Haven Medical Center for twenty-seven years. Currently he is the Robert W. Berliner Emeritus Professor of Medicine and Senior Research Scientist at Yale, where he continues to see patients, teach, write, and mentor. He is recognized for his pioneer research in the development of nuclear cardiology. Dr. Zaret has written or edited five medical texts, one of which is in its fourth edition, as well as several hundred scientific papers and book chapters. He was the founding Editor-in-Chief of the *Journal of Nuclear Cardiology*. He has received many awards for his scientific work and is a member of several honorific societies. Dr. Zaret is also an accomplished painter whose oils appear in numerous private collections. He has exhibited in New Haven and Hartford, Connecticut, as well as in the Berkshires. The father of three and grandfather of six, Barry L. Zaret lives in Woodbridge, CT and East Otis, MA.

This book is set in Garamond Premier Pro, which had its genesis in 1988 when type-designer Robert Slimbach visited the Plantin-Moretus Museum in Antwerp, Belgium, to study its collection of Claude Garamond's metal punches and typefaces. During the mid-fifteen hundreds, Garamond—a Parisian punch-cutter—produced a refined array of book types that combined an unprecedented degree of balance and elegance, for centuries standing as the pinnacle of beauty and practicality in type-founding. Slimbach has created an entirely new interpretation based on Garamond's designs and on comparable italics cut by Robert Granjon, Garamond's contemporary.

To order additional copies of this book
or other Antrim House titles, contact the publisher at

Antrim House
21 Goodrich Rd., Simsbury, CT 06070
860.217.0023, AntrimHouse@comcast.net
or the house website (www.AntrimHouseBooks.com).

•

On the house website
in addition to information on books
you will find sample poems, upcoming events,
and a "seminar room" featuring supplemental biography,
notes, images, poems, reviews, and
writing suggestions.

Made in the USA
Coppell, TX
20 June 2025

50965873R00066